I0426236

Fish Community Monitoring at Wilson's Creek National Battlefield

2006, 2007 and 2010 Status Report

Natural Resource Data Series NPS/HTLN/NRDS—2011/176

Hope R. Dodd

National Park Service
Heartland I&M Network and Prairie Cluster Prototype Monitoring Program
Wilson's Creek National Battlefield
6424 W Farm Road 182
Republic, MO 65738

David E. Bowles

National Park Service
Heartland I&M Network and Prairie Cluster Prototype Monitoring Program
Wilson's Creek National Battlefield
6424 W Farm Road 182
Republic, MO 65738

Samantha K. Mueller

University of Minnesota Duluth
Biology
207 SSB
1035 Kirby Drive
Duluth, MN 55812

Myranda K. Clark

Missouri State University
Biology Department
901 S. National Avenue
Springfield, MO 65897

June 2011

U.S. Department of the Interior
National Park Service
Natural Resource Stewardship and Science
Fort Collins, Colorado

The National Park Service, Natural Resource Stewardship and Science office in Fort Collins, Colorado publishes a range of reports that address natural resource topics of interest and applicability to a broad audience in the National Park Service and others in natural resource management, including scientists, conservation and environmental constituencies, and the public.

The Natural Resource Data Series is intended for the timely release of basic data sets and data summaries. Care has been taken to assure accuracy of raw data values, but a thorough analysis and interpretation of the data has not been completed. Consequently, the initial analyses of data in this report are provisional and subject to change.

All manuscripts in the series receive the appropriate level of peer review to ensure that the information is scientifically credible, technically accurate, appropriately written for the intended audience, and designed and published in a professional manner.

This report received informal peer review by subject-matter experts who were not directly involved in the collection, analysis, or reporting of the data. Data in this report were collected and analyzed using methods based on established, peer-reviewed protocols and were analyzed and interpreted within the guidelines of the protocols.

Views, statements, findings, conclusions, recommendations, and data in this report do not necessarily reflect views and policies of the National Park Service, U.S. Department of the Interior. Mention of trade names or commercial products does not constitute endorsement or recommendation for use by the U.S. Government.

This report is available from (http://science.nature.nps.gov/im/units/htln/) and the Natural Resource Publications Management website (http://www.nature.nps.gov/publications/nrpm/).

Please cite this publication as:

Dodd, H .R., D. E. Bowles, and S. K. Mueller, and M. K. Clark. 2011. Fish community monitoring at Wilson's Creek National Battlefield: 2006-2007, 2010 status report. Natural Resource Data Series NPS/HTLN/NRDS—2011/176. National Park Service, Fort Collins, Colorado.

NPS 410/108051, June 2011

Contents

Figures

Tables

Abstract

In 2006, 2007 and 2010, fish communities, water quality, and physical habitat were sampled at Wilson's Creek, Skegg's Branch (also known as Schuyler Creek), and Terrell Creek to determine the status and long-term trends in fish community composition and to correlate this community data to water quality and habitat conditions. Prior to initiating our long-term monitoring, previous studies of fish communities in Wilson's Creek assessed the water quality and biotic integrity of this urban stream (Donegan 1984, Foster 1988, Foster 1989, Peterson and Justus 2005), but little is known about the fish communities or water quality conditions of Skegg's Branch and Terrell Creek. Based on our data, the fish communities within WICR were found to be diverse. Although water quality has been an issue due to wastewater effluent and runoff from urban areas, Wilson's Creek maintains high species richness, number of intolerant species, and diversity, resulting in a high biotic integrity rating. However, fish assemblages in Wilson's Creek did show a higher number of anomalies (disease, eroded fins, lesions, tumors, and blackspot parasite) in 2010 compared to communities in the other two streams sampled. The high quality fish community in Wilson's Creek can be misleading because anthropogenic disturbances as well as abiotic factors are likely the explanation for these findings. Skegg's Branch and Terrell Creek rated as having good biotic integrity and had a large proportion of the community made up of darter, sculpin, and madtom species (sensitive to siltation and poor water quality) in 2007 and 2010, suggesting that these two smaller tributaries of Wilson's Creek are in good condition.

Acknowledgments

We would like to thank Tyler Cribbs and Jan Hinsey from Heartland I&M Network, Jake Waters and Jessica Lurras from Missouri State University, and Shawn Hodges from Buffalo National River for assistance with field work. Also, thanks to Jen Haack (Heartland I&M Network) for GPS/GIS assistance. We would like to acknowledge the staff at Wilson's Creek National Battlefield for their support.

Introduction

Wilson's Creek National Battlefield (WICR) contains portions of three perennial streams: Wilson's Creek, Skegg's Branch (also named Schuyler Creek), and Terrell Creek (Figure 1). All three streams are influenced by springs, but have varying degrees of urban and agricultural land use within their watersheds. Wilson's Creek is an urban stream whose watershed drains the city of Springfield, Missouri, with a majority of its flow below Rader Spring consisting of effluent from a wastewater treatment facility. Historically, both point-source and non-point source pollution in Wilson's Creek and its tributaries created low dissolved oxygen conditions (Emmett et al. 1978) unsuitable for aquatic biota. Improvements to the wastewater treatment facility improved water quality (Consoer et al. 1980) resulting in a moderately diverse fish community (Donegan 1984, Foster 1988, Foster 1989). However, due to non-point pollution from urban and rural sources in the Wilson's Creek watershed, this stream has been listed on the Missouri Department of Natural Resources 303(d) list for bacterial contamination and unknown pollutants (http://dnr.mo.gov/env/wpp/waterquality/303d/090810-cwc-approved-303d.pdf). The Skegg's Branch watershed consists largely of rural land use. However, its headwaters are located in the town of Republic, Missouri, which has shown tremendous development and population growth in the last decade. The summer base flow of Skegg's Branch is largely derived from Campground Spring, located downstream of Republic, Missouri. Therefore, the expansion of this town may lead to declines in water quality and biotic integrity of both Campground Spring and Skegg's Branch. Land use in the Terrell Creek watershed is predominately agricultural (hay and cattle), although this watershed also drains from both a golf course and a quarry. Double Spring, located within the park, contributes most of Terrell Creek's base flow during summer months. Upstream of the spring, Terrell Creek becomes intermittent during years of low precipitation.

Previous studies of fish communities in Wilson's Creek have been used to assess the water quality and biotic integrity of this stream (Donegan 1984, Foster 1988, Foster 1989, Peterson and Justus 2005), but little is known about the fish communities or water quality conditions of Skegg's Branch and Terrell Creek. Fish communities are an important component of Ozark stream systems. Because changes or shifts in stream habitat complexity and water quality often determine biotic communities, including fish (Lazorchak et al. 1998), monitoring trends in fish community composition along with associated habitat conditions serves as a strong basis for measuring stream integrity. Many fish species are considered intolerant of habitat alterations and monitoring their assemblages can serve as a useful tool to assess changes in water and habitat quality (Karr 1981; Robison and Buchanan 1988; Pflieger 1997; Barbour et al. 1999; Peitz 2005). Moreover, the intrinsic value of fish to the public as environmental indicators and as a recreational opportunity makes the status of fish diversity a valuable interpretive topic for park visitors and an informative tool for monitoring the status of aquatic resources at WICR.

Objectives of fish community monitoring at WICR are: (1) to determine the status and long term trends in fish richness, diversity, abundance, and community composition and (2) to correlate the long-term community data to overall water quality and habitat condition.

Methods

Details on methods of site selection, fish sampling, and habitat and water quality data collection not listed in this report can be found in the Protocol for Monitoring Fish Communities in Small Streams in the Heartland Inventory and Monitoring Network (Dodd *et al.* 2008).

Study Area and Site Selection
Portions of three wadeable streams run through WICR: Wilson's Creek (~ 5.3 km), Skegg's Branch (~0.9 km), and Terrell Creek (~ 1.7 km). Sampling reaches were selected at the downstream end of each stream either near the park boundary (for Wilson's Creek) or upstream of the confluence with another stream, Skegg's Branch (Figure 1). Terrell Creek, which is also a tributary to Wilson's Creek, was sampled upstream of Highway ZZ bridge to avoid the localized influence of this structure on channel morphology and fish habitat. Reach length was defined as 20 times the mean wetted stream width (MWSW) with a minimum of 150 m, allowing inclusion of representative channel units (riffle, run, and pool habitats) located within the stream (Moulton *et al.*, 2002).

Fish Collection
Fish communities were sampled in June of 2006 and May of 2007 and 2010. Fish were collected throughout the reach using a single pass with a pulsed DC backpack electrofishing unit in Skegg's Branch and Terrell Creek and a pulsed DC tow barge unit in Wilson's Creek. During sampling, fish were collected with nets and placed in aerated buckets. All fish were identified to species, if possible, and counted. A subsample of 30 individuals per species were measured and weighed, and any anomalies (deformities, eroded fins, lesions, tumors, and blackspot parasite) were recorded. Fish that were too small or that were difficult to identify in the field were preserved for laboratory identification. All other fish were released back into the sample reach.

Habitat and Water Quality
Physical habitat and water quality data were collected in conjunction with fish sampling. An 11 transect method was used to collect data on general channel morphology, fish cover, and bank conditions within the entire reach. In-stream habitat (depth, velocity, substrate, *etc.*) and fish cover (presence of boulders, hydrophytes, *etc.*) were assessed at three points per transect (see Dodd *et al.* (2008), SOP #5 for a list of all habitat parameters collected). Fish cover along the banks (undercut banks, overhanging terrestrial vegetation, *etc.*) and bank/riparian stability were assessed on the left and right banks at each transect. Hourly water quality data (temperature, dissolved oxygen, pH, specific conductance, and turbidity) was collected using loggers deployed near the reach for at least 24 hours.

Data Analysis
Biological metrics were calculated for each reach sampled in 2006-2007 and 2010. These metrics reflect fish community diversity (species richness and Simpson's Diversity Index), abundance (catch per unit effort), composition (number and percent composition of sensitive taxa), and overall stream integrity (Index of Biotic Integrity). Community diversity was assessed using Simpson's Diversity Index, which gives the probability that two individuals picked at random from the site are the same species. Therefore, the index decreases with increasing diversity and ranges from 0 (completely diverse) to 1 (no diversity). For community composition, number and percent composition of sucker (Catastomidae), sunfish (Centrarchidae; excluding Bluegill

(*Lepomis macrochirus*) and Green sunfish (L. cyanellus)), and darter/sculpin/madtom (*Etheostoma* and *Percina/Cottus/Noturus*) species were calculated because these metrics are typically used in several Index of Biotic Integrity (IBI) calculations (Karr 1981, Dauwalter *et al.* 2003, Smogor 2005) and demonstrate sensitivity to human disturbance. The IBI developed by Dauwalter *et al.* (2003) was used to assess overall stream health and includes seven metrics: 1) percent of individuals as algivorous/herbivorous, invertivorous, and piscivorous; 2) percent with an anomaly (disease, eroded fins, lesions, or tumors) or blackspot parasite; 3) percent as green sunfish (*Lepomis cyanellus*), bluegill (*Lepomis macrochirus*), yellow bullhead (*Ameiurus natalis*), or channel catfish (*Ictalurus punctatus*); 4) percent invertivores; 5) percent top carnivores; 6) number of darter/sculpin/madtom species; 7) number of lithophilic (sand/gravel) spawning species. Each of the seven raw metric values was scored from 0 to 10 based on upper and lower thresholds developed for the Ozarks region. Metric scores were summed to calculate an IBI score that ranges from 0 to 100. Based on this IBI score, the overall integrity of the stream is classified from very poor to excellent: very poor = 0-20; poor = 20-40; fair = 40-60; good = 60-80; excellent (reference condition) = 80-100. More detailed methods on calculating biological metrics used in this report can be found in Dauwalter *et al.* (2003).

Physical habitat and water quality data were summarized using averages with standard errors (SE) or percentages, where appropriate. Physical habitat data were summarized as in-stream habitat, fish cover, and bank stability. For in-stream substrate data, the Wentworth code for particle sizes (see SOP #5 in Dodd *et al.* 2008 for the code categories and size ranges) were used. For assessment of stream banks, categories of bank angle, percent vegetation, height, and substrate were used to assess overall bank stability. Water quality data were summarized using averages and standard errors.

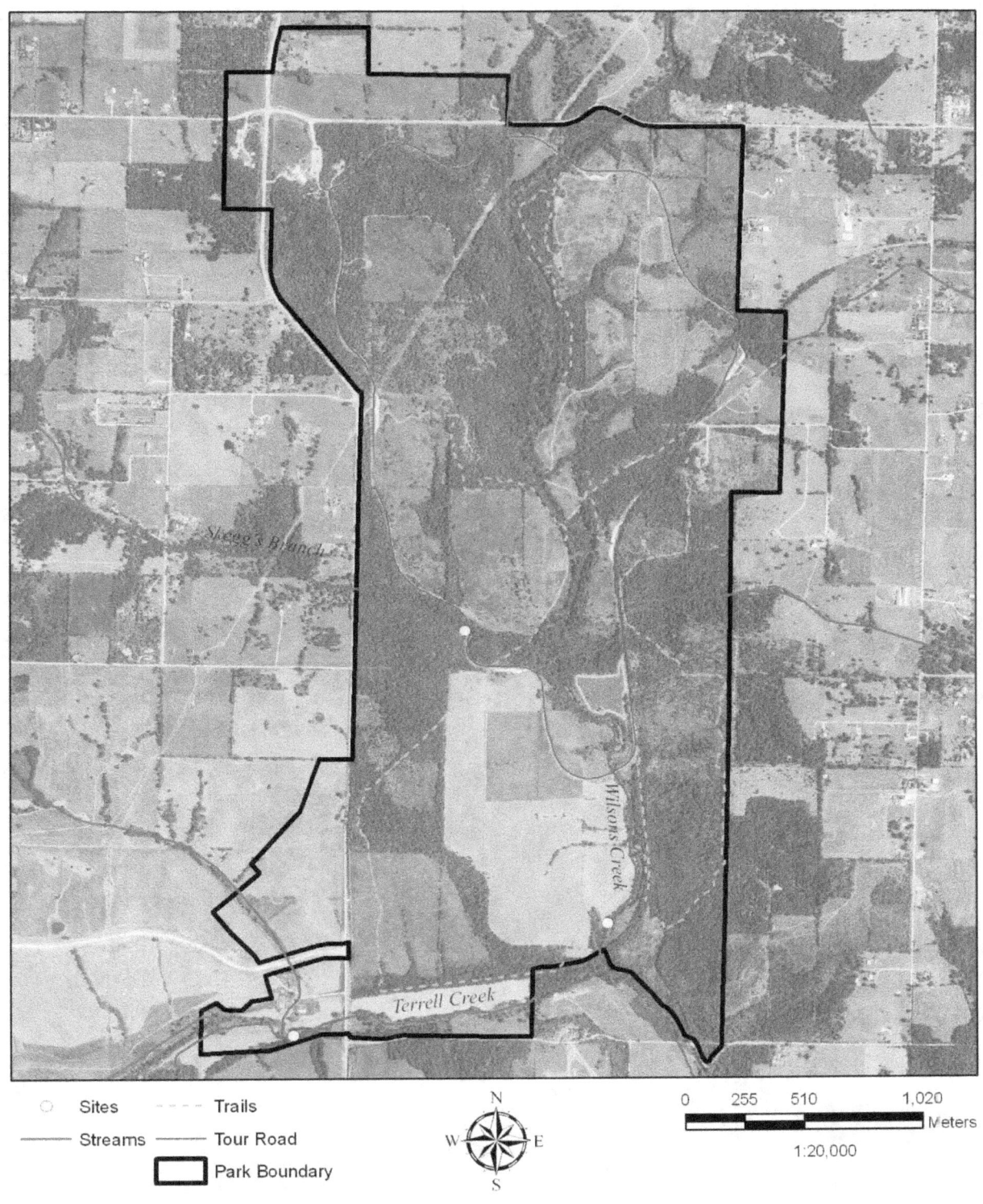

Figure 1. Location of fish monitoring sites at WICR.

Results

Fish Community

Species richness (i.e., number of species) among all sites ranged from 9 to 27 in 2006, 8 to 24 in 2007, and 8 to 23 in 2010 (Figure 2, top panel). Wilson's Creek, the largest of the three streams, had the highest number of species in each year. Skegg's Branch had the lowest species richness in all years sampled. Simpson's Diversity Index ranged from 0.09 to 0.31 at Wilson's Creek, 0.16 to 0.43 at Skegg's Branch, and 0.26 to 0.73 at Terrell Creek (Figure 2, middle panel). Diversity was highest at Wilson's Creek (i.e., low Simpson's Index) in all years sampled and lowest at Terrell Creek (i.e., high Simpson's Index) in 2007 and 2010. Terrell Creek showed the greatest variability in diversity across years. Fish abundance ranged from 8 to 15 fish/min at Wilson's Creek, 10 to 28 fish/min at Skegg's Branch, and 10 to 13 fish/min at Terrell Creek (Figure 2, bottom panel). At all sites, abundance was lowest in 2007. Skegg's Branch had the highest variability in abundance due to high numbers of Stoneroller species (*Campostoma spp.*) in 2006 and Ozark sculpins (*Cottus hypselurus*) in 2010, while Terrell Creek had the lowest variability among years. All three streams showed a decrease in numbers of Stoneroller spp. (a species tolerant to disturbance) and an increase in numbers of Ozark sculpin (a species sensitive to siltation and poor water quality) from 2006 to 2010 (Appendix 1). In addition to having relatively high numbers of species and relatively high diversity, Wilson's Creek also had the highest number of species intolerant to human disturbance (siltation, poor water quality, etc.), ranging from 11 to 13 species. Number of intolerant species at Terrell Creek ranged from 4 to 6 species. Skegg's Branch had 4 to 5 intolerant species present.

In general, Wilson's Creek had higher numbers and percent composition of sucker, sunfish (excluding the tolerant Bluegill and Green sunfish species) and dartetr/sculpin/madtom species compared to its two smaller tributaries (Table 1). Skegg's Branch, the smallest of the two tributaries, had no sunfish or sucker species present. IBI scores ranged from 73 to 98 at Wilson's Creek, 61 to 73 at Skegg's Branch, and 60 to 63 at Terrell Creek (Figure 3, Table 2). Skegg's Branch and Terrell Creek rated as having "good" biotic integrity in all years sampled. Wilson's Creek rated as "excellent" in 2006 and 2007 and rated as "good" in 2010. Higher IBI scores for Wilson's Creek compared to the tributaries is likely due to the higher percentage of invertivores and higher numbers of darters/sculpins/madtoms species and lithophilic (require clean gravel) spawners. The decline in IBI score for Wilson's Creek in 2010 is due to the increase in fish with anomalies and a decrease in invertivorous fish.

Habitat and Water Quality

Wilson's Creek was wider, deeper, and had more flow than its two tributary streams (Table 3). Skegg's Branch was the smallest and had the least amount of flow of the three streams. All streams deeper with higher velocity and discharge in 2007. Substrate in Wilson's Creek and Skegg's Branch consisted of small to large pebble (Wentworth sizes 12-14, 16.0-45 mm). Terrell Creek consisted of slightly smaller substrates of course gravel to small pebble (Wentworth sizes 11-13, 11.3-32.0 mm).

Fish cover in WICR streams was primarily small woody debris, filamentous algae, and aquatic plants and mosses (hydrophytes). Because several cover types may be present at a transect, the percentages given are percent of the reach that contain each cover type; therefore percentages do not add to 100% for the reach. All three streams had over half of their area covered by small woody debris in each year sampled (Wilson's Creek 55-67%, Skegg's Branch 67%, and Terrell Creek 61-64%). Wilson's Creek also had 61% of its area covered by filamentous algae in 2007 and 55% covered by hydrophytes in 2010. The stream bottom at Skegg's Branch was also covered by filamentous algae (94%) in 2007 and by hydrophytes in 2006 (67%). The sampled area of Terrell Creek was largely covered by hydrophytes in 2006 (64%) and by filamentous algae in 2010 (79%) and by both cover types (hydrophytes = 58%, filamentous algae = 79%) in 2007. The hydrophytes in Skegg's Branch and Wilson's Creek were dominated by mosses in comparison to Terrell Creek where other aquatic plants were dominant.

Banks were relatively stable for Terrell and Skegg's Branch, while Wilson's Creek had higher and steeper banks that were less stable (Table 4). A large percentage of banks at Terrell Creek had angles less than 60°, vegetation cover greater than 80%, and bank heights less than 2 m, but did consist largely of erodible silt substrate. Skegg's Branch had a higher percentage of the banks greater than a 60° angle with less vegetation (larger percentage of banks with 50-80% cover) than banks in Terrell Creek; however, this stream also had a higher percent of bedrock and cobble/boulder substrate, a more stable substrate than silt. Wilson's Creek had the least stable banks of the three streams sampled in the park. In all years, a high percentage of the banks (63.6 – 86.4%) were greater than a 60° angle and were greater than 2 m in height, indicating a higher potential for bank erosion. Percentage of bank vegetation cover at Wilson's Creek was similar to Terrell Creek and substrate sizes were similar to Skegg's Branch. Measurements of bank stability, particularly bank height and bank substrate, showed large changes among years within particular stream reaches (Table 4). Considerable changes in bank characteristics would be expected if flooding or significant alterations in riparian land use occurred. Due to the urban land use within Wilson's Creek watershed, this stream is flashy (rapid rises and decreases of flow) during storm events, and it is possible that bank characteristics in this stream may change dramatically among years. However, large changes in bank characteristics for both Skegg's Branch and Terrell Creek, which have far less urban land use in their watersheds and are less flashy, is likely due to a result of observational sampling methods rather than a true change in bank stability. Further analysis of bank measurement data is warranted to determine the validity of using observational sampling methods to assess bank stability.

Wilson's Creek typically had higher water temperatures, specific conductance, and turbidity than its two tributaries (Table 5), likely due to a more open canopy and the influence of urban runoff and wastewater treatment effluent. Skegg's Branch and Terrell Creek, which are heavily influenced by springs that are located in or near the park, had lower water temperatures. Temperatures were warmer in 2006 in all streams, due to sampling occurring in June that year. Average dissolved oxygen was highest in 2010 for all streams, possibly due to low water temperatures, with Wilson's Creek showing larger diel fluctuations (range: 7.5-13.1 mg/L). pH was relatively stable among years and similar between the three streams.

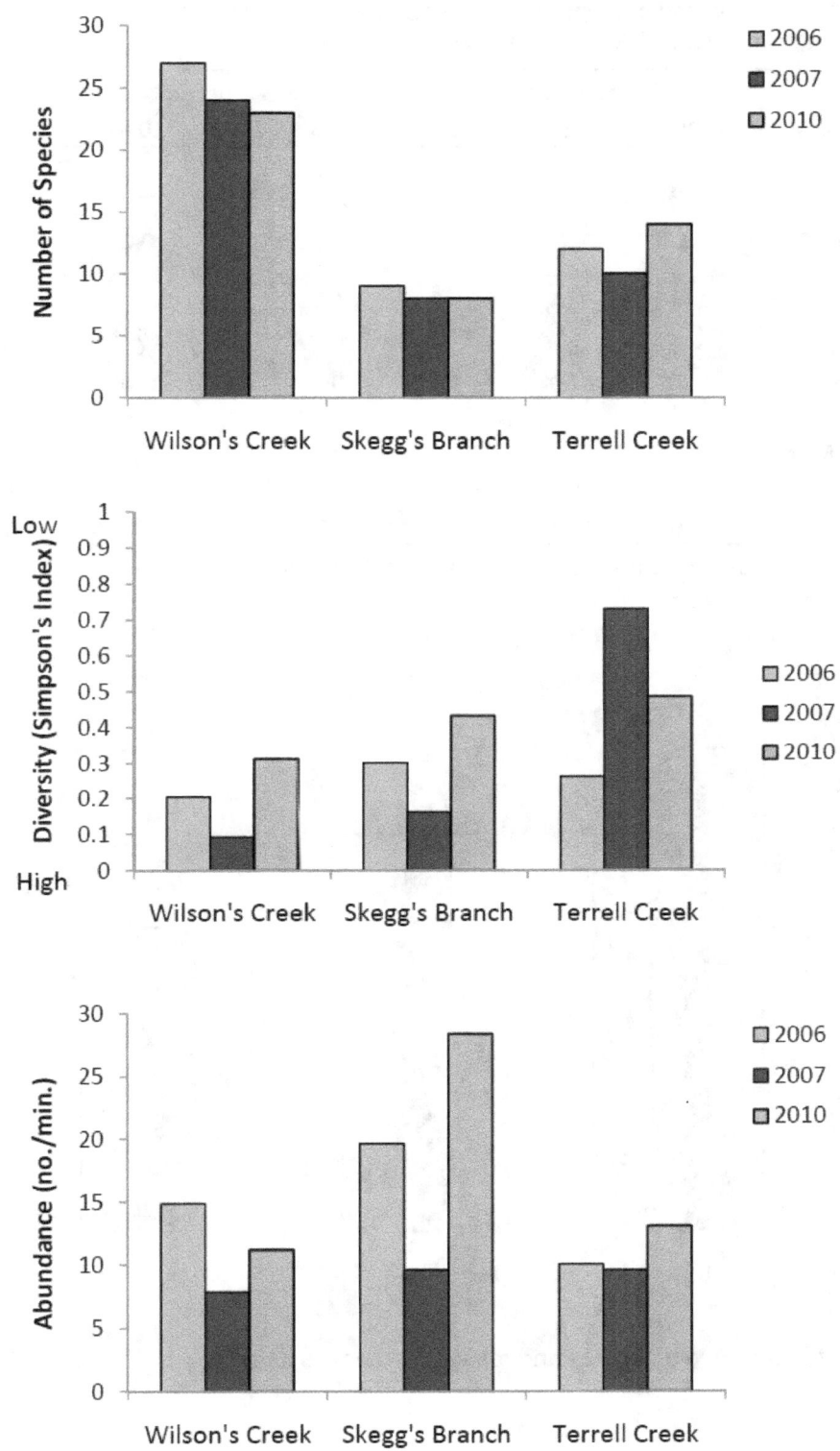

Figure 2. Species richness, community diversity (Simpson's Index), and abundance for reaches sampled at WICR in 2006, 2007, and 2010.

Table 1. Number of species and percent composition of sucker, sunfish, and sculpin/madtom/darter species for reaches sampled in 2006, 2007, and 2010.

Composition Metric	Wilson's Creek			Skegg's Branch			Terrell Creek		
	2006	2007	2010	2006	2007	2010	2006	2007	2010
Suckers									
No. of Species	2	3	3	0	0	0	1	1	2
% Composition	1.3	1.2	7.5	0	0	0.0	2.6	0.4	0.8
Sunfish									
No. of Species*	2	3	3	0	0	0	0	0	3
% Composition*	4.2	17.9	13.3	0	0	0.0	0	0	0.5
Darter/Sculpin/Madtom									
No. of Species	8	8	8	4	5	4	3	4	5
% Composition	19.1	49.1	66.4	15.7	52.9	69.6	32.9	90.4	81.1

*Excludes Bluegill and Green sunfish (species tolerant to poor water quality)

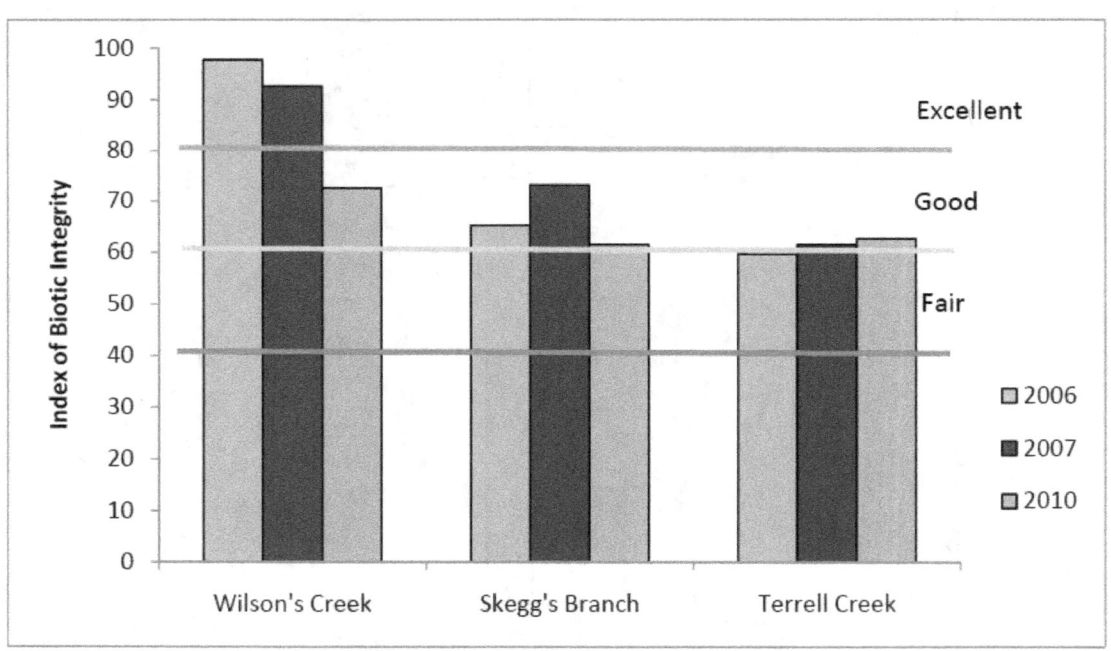

Figure 3. Index of Biotic Integrity scores and ratings for reaches sampled at WICR in 2006, 2007, and 2010.

Table 2. Index of Biotic Integrity (IBI) scores and metric values for each reach sampled in 2006, 2007, and 2010. AHIP = individuals that are Algivorous, Herbivorous, Invertivorous, and Piscivorous, Anomaly = individuals with a disease, eroded fins, lesions, tumors, or blackspot,, GBYC = individuals as Green sunfish, Bluegill, Yellow bullhead, or Channel catfish, DSM = Darter/Sculpin/Madtom species, Lithophilic = species that are sand/gravel spawners.

Metric	Wilson's Creek			Skegg's Branch			Terrell Creek		
	2006	2007	2010	2006	2007	2010	2006	2007	2010
% AHIP	0.5	3.6	2.6	0.0	0.0	0.0	0.0	0.0	0.6
% Anomaly	0.0	0.0	1.7	0.0	0.0	0.2	0.0	0.0	0.2
% GBYC	0.6	3.8	4.7	0.0	0.0	0.0	0.1	0.0	4.0
% Invertivorous	35.3	42.8	23.8	9.5	24.3	3.8	5.8	1.7	5.2
% Top Carnivore	3.0	8.2	5.1	0.0	0.0	0.0	0.0	0.0	0.0
No. DSM Species	8	8	8	4	5	4	3	4	5
No. Lithophilic Species	18	17	16	8	8	8	8	9	11
IBI	98	93	73	65	73	61	60	61	63

Table 3. Average width, depth, velocity, and substrate (one standard error) and total discharge for each reach sampled in 2006, 2007, and 2010.

Habitat Metric	Wilson's Creek			Skegg's Branch			Terrell Creek		
	2006	2007	2010	2006	2007	2010	2006	2007	2010
Average Width (m)	15.4 (0.5)	17.4 (0.4)	16.5 (0.6)	5.1 (0.2)	6.2 (0.2)	6.2 (0.6)	10.6 (0.4)	10.4 (0.4)	9.8 (0.9)
Average Depth (cm)	46.2 (4.0)	58.5 (4.0)	54.3 (4.4)	10.5 (2.0)	19.9 (2.2)	17.7 (1.8)	34.3 (3.4)	39.0 (3.8)	37.8 (3.4)
Average Velocity (m/s)	0.31 (0.04)	0.49 (0.04)	0.42 (0.04)	0.06 (0.01)	0.19 (0.02)	0.16 (0.02)	0.04 (0.01)	0.21 (0.03)	0.17 (0.03)
Substrate (Wentworth)	13.2 (0.6)	12.6 (0.7)	14.0 (0.8)	13.6 (0.4)	14.1 (0.4)	13.2 (0.5)	11.2 (0.9)	12.7 (0.7)	13.0 (0.5)
Discharge (m^3/s)	0.93	3.74	2.30	0.01	0.13	0.10	0.10	0.47	0.33

Table 4. Bank angle, vegetation, height, and substrate characteristics (in percent of total bank) for each reach sampled in 2006, 2007, and 2010.

	Wilson's Creek			Skegg's Branch			Terrell Creek		
	2006	2007	2010	2006	2007	2010	2006	2007	2010
Angle									
< 60°	13.6	18.2	36.4	45.5	45.5	31.8	68.2	72.7	59.1
> 60°	86.4	81.8	63.6	54.5	54.5	63.6	31.8	27.3	40.9
Vegetation									
>80%	90.9	100.0	81.8	54.5	81.8	81.8	100.0	86.4	90.9
50-80%	4.5	0.0	18.2	31.8	18.2	18.2	0.0	13.6	9.1
<50%	4.5	0.0	0.0	13.6	0.0	0.0	0.0	0.0	0.0
Height									
<1m	0.0	45.5	0.0	4.5	0.0	13.6	45.5	9.1	18.2
1-2m	18.2	50.0	9.1	63.6	54.5	54.5	36.4	40.9	50.0
2-3m	18.2	4.5	63.6	0.0	31.8	18.2	0.0	27.3	9.1
>3m	63.6	0.0	27.3	31.8	13.6	13.6	18.2	22.7	22.7
Substrate									
Silt	54.5	59.1	40.9	0.0	59.1	31.8	100.0	77.3	27.3
Sand/Gravel	22.7	13.6	36.4	63.6	9.1	45.5	0.0	4.5	54.5
Cobble/Boulder	18.2	13.6	0.0	13.6	13.6	0.0	0.0	13.6	13.6
Bedrock	4.5	13.6	22.7	22.7	18.2	22.7	0.0	4.5	4.5

Table 5. Average water quality parameters (one standard error) for each reach sampled in 2006, 2007, and 2010. NC = parameter not collected. An asterisk indicates a possible error in parameter readings due to faulty meter, and therefore, no data is reported.

Water Quality Parameter	Wilson's Creek			Skegg's Branch			Terrell Creek		
	2006	2007	2010	2006	2007	2010	2006	2007	2010
Ave. Water Temperature (°C)	22.5 (0.1)	18.5 (0.3)	18.1 (0.3)	18.7 (0.2)	15.3 (0.1)	14.5 (0.2)	16.3 (0.1)	14.7 (0.1)	14.1 (0.2)
Ave. pH	7.77 (0.01)	*	7.93 (0.03)	7.92 (0.01)	*	7.72 (0.01)	7.38 (0.01)	*	7.64 (0.01)
Ave. Specific Conductance (μS/cm)	486.5 (4.4)	643.0 (2.8)	775.7 (4.1)	495.8 (0.6)	489.5 (0.0)	455.6 (0.47)	471.7 (0.2)	477.6 (0.0)	413.4 (0.2)
Ave. Dissolved Oxygen (mg/L)	9.16 (0.12)	NC	9.39 (0.38)	8.82 (0.1)	NC	11.08 (0.17)	8.98 (0.15)	6.45 (0.12)	9.70 (0.15)
Ave. Turbidity (NTU)	9.57 (2.39)	4.25 (0.13)	1.30 (0.04)	0.69 (0.05)	2.07 (0.07)	0.00 (0.05)	2.70 (0.22)	0.76 (0.04)	0.91 (0.16)

14

Discussion

Fish communities within WICR are diverse as evidenced by the numerous species present, high composition of sensitive darter, sculpin, and madtom species, and good IBI score ratings. Although water quality has been an issue due to wastewater effluent and runoff from urban areas, Wilson's Creek has high species richness, number of intolerant species, and diversity, resulting in a high biotic integrity rating. However, the high quality fish community in Wilson's Creek can be misleading because anthropogenic disturbances as well as abiotic factors are likely the explanation for these findings. The larger size of Wilson's Creek, compared to the smaller tributaries in the park, would allow for both larger species (suckers, sunfish, and bass) as well as smaller species to inhabit this stream. In addition, Wilson's Creek is likely a more productive system than the other streams within the park because of the upstream inputs of nitrogen and phosphorus from the wastewater treatment facility. While a highly productive system can create a food-rich environment for fish and increase species richness and fish abundance, this nutrient rich system can also create major algae blooms, causing daily dissolved oxygen levels to fluctuate substantially. During our late spring/early summer sampling, Wilson's Creek demonstrated larger fluctuations (i.e. larger range) in dissolved oxygen compared to Skegg's Branch or Terrell Creek. By late summer, higher water temperatures and lower water levels could increase diel fluctuations in dissolved oxygen, adding stress to the fish communities in Wilson's Creek. In 2010, the fish communities in Wilson's Creek also showed a higher number of anomalies (disease, eroded fins, lesions, tumors, and blackspot parasite) compared to communities in Skegg's Branch and Terrell Creek. Although Skegg's Branch and Terrell Creek had fewer species, fewer intolerant species, and lower diversity than Wilson's Creek, these streams rated as having good biotic integrity and had a large proportion of the community made up of sensitive darter, sculpin, and madtom species (particularly Ozark sculpins) in 2007 and 2010. The reason for lower richness and diversity in these two tributaries is possibly due to their smaller size and the influence of springs creating cooler water temperatures (~3-6 °C lower than Wilson's Creek). In general, spring-dominated streams generally have a lower diversity in comparison to surface water streams. Overall, fish communities at WICR are in good condition. Although nutrient enrichment and bacterial contamination are issues for Wilson's Creek, this stream has a diverse community.

Literature Cited

Barbour, M. T., J. Gerritsen, B. D. Snyder, and J. B. Stribling. 1999. Rapid bioassessment protocols for use in streams and wadeable rivers: periphyton, benthic macroinvertebrate, and fish, 2nd edition. EPA 841-B-99-002, U.S. Environmental Protection Agency, Washington, DC.

Consoer, Townsend and Associates, Consulting Engineers. 1980. Waste load allocation study: James River – Wilson Creek, Little Sac River – South dry Sac Creek. Report to Missouri Department of Natural Resources, Jefferson City, Missouri.

Dauwalter, D. C., E. J. Pert, and W. E. Keith. 2003. An index of biotic integrity for fish assemblages in Ozark Highland Streams of Arkansas. *Southeastern Naturalist* 2:447-468.

Dodd, H. R., D. G. Peitz, G. A. Rowell, D. E. Bowles, and L. M. Morrison. 2008. Protocol for monitoring fish communities in small streams in the Heartland Inventory and Monitoring Network. Natural Resource Report NPS/HTLN/NRR—2008/052. National Park Service, Fort Collins, Colorado.

Donegon, D.S. 1984. Wilson's Creek fish species diversity. Wilson's Creek Natural Resource Survey Unpublished report, Republic, Missouri.

Doppelt, B. M, C. Scurlock, and J. Karr. 1993. Entering the watershed: a new approach to save America's river ecosystems. Island Press, Washington, DC.

Emmett, L. F., J. Skelton, R. R. Luckey, D. E. Miller, T. L. Thompson, and J. W. Whitfield. 1978. Water resources and geology of the Springfield area, Missouri. Missouri Department of Natural Resources, Division of Geology and Land Survey, Water Resources Report 34.

Foster, D. 1988. Fish survey of Wilson's Creek. National Park Service, Ozark National Scenic Riverways, Van Buren, MO.

Foster, D. 1989. Fish survey of Wilson's Creek. National Park Service, Ozark National Scenic Riverways, Van Buren, MO.

Karr J. R. 1981. Assessment of biotic integrity using fish communities. *Fisheries* 6:21–27.

Lazorchak, J. M., Klemm, D. J., and D. V. Peck. 1998. Environmental monitoring and assessment program-surface waters: field operations and methods for measuring the ecological condition of wadeable streams. EPA/620/R-94/004F. U.S. Environmental Protection Agency, Washington, DC.

Missouri Department of Natural Resources. 2010. 303(d) list as approved by the Missouri Clean Water Commission. Available at: http://dnr.mo.gov/env/wpp/waterquality/303d/090810-cwc-approved-303d.pdf (accessed March 2011)

Moulton, S. R. III, J. G. Kennen, R. M. Goldstein, and J. A. Hambrook. 2002. Revised protocols for sampling algal, invertebrate, and fish communities as part of the National Water-Quality Assessment Program. U.S. Geological Survey, Reston, Virginia. Open-file Report 02-150.

Osborne, L.L., and D.A. Kovacic. 1993. Riparian vegetated buffer strips in water-quality restoration and stream management. Freshwater Biology 29:243-258.

Peitz, D.G. 2005. Fish community monitoring in prairie park streams with emphasis on Topeka shiner (*Notropis Topeka*): summary report 2001-2004. National Park Service, Fort Collins, Colorado.

Peterjohn, W.T., and D.L. Correll. 1984. Nutrient dynamics in an agricultural watershed: observations on the role of a riparian forest. Ecology 65:1466-1475.

Petersen, J.C. and B.G. Justus. 2005. The fishes of Wilson's Creek National Battlefield, Missouri, 2003. U.S. Geological Survey, Little Rock, AR. Scientific Investigations Report 2005-5127

Pflieger, W. L. 1997. The fishes of Missouri. Missouri Department of Conservation, Jefferson City, Missouri.

Robison, H. W., and T. M. Buchanan. 1988. Fishes of Arkansas. University of Arkansas Press, Fayetteville, AR.

Smogor, R. 2005. Draft manual for interpreting Illinois fish IBI scores. Illinois Environmental Protection Agency, Bureau of Water, Surface Water Section.

Stauffer, J.C. R.M. Goldstein, and R.M. Newman. 2000. Relationship of wooded riparian zones and runoff potential to fish community composition in agricultural streams. Canadian Journal of Fisheries and Aquatic Sciences 57:307-316.

Appendix

Appendix 1. List of species and number collected at WICR in 2006, 2007, and 2010. Asterisk denotes intolerant fish species.

Family	Common Name	Scientific Name	2006	2007	2010
Wilson's Creek					
Catostomidae	Black redhorse*	*Moxostoma duquesnei*	0	3	34
Catostomidae	Golden redhorse	*Moxostoma erythrurum*	13	1	9
Catostomidae	Northern hog sucker*	*Hypentelium nigricans*	9	3	17
Centrarchidae	Bluegill	*Lepomis macrochirus*	0	1	9
Centrarchidae	Green sunfish	*Lepomis cyanellus*	2	1	17
Centrarchidae	Longear sunfish	*Lepomis megalotis*	20	56	73
Centrarchidae	Ozark bass*	*Ambloplites constellatus*	47	47	28
Centrarchidae	Smallmouth bass*	*Micropterus dolomieu*	1	1	6
Cottidae	Banded sculpin*	*Cottus carolinae*	21	11	32
Cottidae	Ozark sculpin*	*Cottus hypselurus*	49	90	437
Cyprinidae	Bluntnose minnow	*Pimephales notatus*	2	0	0
Cyprinidae	Carmine shiner*	*Notropis percobromus*	37	0	1
Cyprinidae	Creek chub	*Semotilus atromaculatus*	39	16	0
Cyprinidae	Duskystripe shiner*	*Luxilus pilsbryi*	45	61	28
Cyprinidae	Luxilus spp.	*Luxilus spp.*	308	0	0
Cyprinidae	Non-carp minnow spp.	*Cyprinidae spp.*	87	0	0
Cyprinidae	Ozark minnow*	*Notropis nubilus*	2	1	0
Cyprinidae	Southern redbelly dace*	*Phoxinus erythrogaster*	38	8	0
Cyprinidae	Stoneroller spp.	*Campostoma spp.*	645	70	10
Cyprinidae	Striped shiner	Luxilus chrysocephalus	1	0	1
Fundulidae	Blackspotted topminnow	*Fundulus olivaceus*	8	5	18
Ictaluridae	Yellow bullhead	*Ameiurus natalis*	8	20	12
Lepisosteidae	Longnose gar	Lepisosteus osseus	0	0	7
Percidae	Banded darter*	*Etheostoma zonale*	24	9	13
Percidae	Greenside darter*	*Etheostoma blennioides*	23	43	14
Percidae	Logperch	*Percina caprodes*	0	1	3
Percidae	Orangethroat darter	*Etheostoma spectabile*	111	26	10
Percidae	Rainbow darter	*Etheostoma caeruleum*	39	63	23
Percidae	Stippled darter*	*Etheostoma punctulatum*	46	43	2
Percidae	Yoke darter*	*Etheostoma juliae*	1	0	0
Poeciliidae	Mosquitofish	*Gambusia affinis*	15	2	0

Appendix 1. cont.

Family	Common Name	Scientific Name	2006	2007	2010
Skegg's Branch					
Cottidae	Banded sculpin*	*Cottus carolinae*	10	31	24
Cottidae	Ozark sculpin*	*Cottus hypselurus*	21	67	390
Cyprinidae	Creek chub	*Semotilus atromaculatus*	72	63	12
Cyprinidae	Duskystripe shiner*	*Luxilus pilsbryi*	1	0	12
Cyprinidae	Non-carp minnow spp.	*Cyprinidae spp.*	2	0	0
Cyprinidae	Southern redbelly dace*	*Phoxinus erythrogaster*	240	29	130
Cyprinidae	Stoneroller spp.	*Campostoma spp.*	110	69	37
Percidae	Orangethroat darter	*Etheostoma spectabile*	31	60	11
Percidae	Rainbow darter	*Etheostoma caeruleum*	0	20	13
Percidae	Stippled darter*	*Etheostoma punctulatum*	17	3	0
Terrell Creek					
Catostomidae	Northern hog sucker*	*Hypentelium nigricans*	0	0	1
Catostomidae	White sucker	*Catostomus commersoni*	20	2	4
Centrarchidae	Bluegill	*Lepomis macrochirus*	0	0	4
Centrarchidae	Green sunfish	*Lepomis cyanellus*	1	0	21
Centrarchidae	Longear sunfish	*Lepomis megalotis*	0	0	3
Cottidae	Banded sculpin*	*Cottus carolinae*	16	19	59
Cottidae	Ozark sculpin*	*Cottus hypselurus*	204	406	427
Cyprinidae	Bluntnose minnow	*Pimephales notatus*	1	0	0
Cyprinidae	Creek chub	*Semotilus atromaculatus*	17	1	5
Cyprinidae	Duskystripe shiner*	*Luxilus pilsbryi*	13	4	22
Cyprinidae	Southern redbelly dace*	*Phoxinus erythrogaster*	283	32	14
Cyprinidae	Stoneroller spp.	*Campostoma spp.*	161	5	39
Fundulidae	Blackspotted topminnow	*Fundulus olivaceus*	10	2	0
Percidae	Greenside darter*	*Etheostoma blennioides*	0	0	1
Percidae	Orangethroat darter	*Etheostoma spectabile*	34	5	11
Percidae	Rainbow darter	*Etheostoma caeruleum*	0	0	12
Percidae	Stippled darter*	*Etheostoma punctulatum*	0	1	0
Poeciliidae	Mosquitofish	*Gambusia affinis*	3	0	0